Ancient Greek Warfare

By Rob S. Rice

Please visit our Web site at www.garethstevens.com
For a free color catalog describing Gareth Stevens Publishing's
list of high-quality books call 1-800-542-2595 (USA)
or 1-800-387-3187 (Canada).
Gareth Stevens Publishing's fax: 1-877-542-2596

Library of Congress Cataloging-in-Publication Data

Rice, Rob S.
    Ancient Greek Warfare / by Rob S. Rice.
        p. cm. — (Ancient Warfare)
    Includes bibliographical references and index.
    ISBN-10: 1-4339-1972-9   (lib. bdg.)
    ISBN-13: 978-1-4339-1972-5   (lib. bdg.)
  1. Military art and science—Greece-History—To 1500—Juvenile literature.
2. Greece—History, Military—To 146 B.C.—Juvenile literature.   3. Military art and
science—History To 500—Juvenile literature.   4. Military history, Ancient—Juvenile
literature. I. Title.
U33.R53   2009
355.020938—DC22   2009006198

This North American edition first published in 2010 by
GS Learning Library
1 Reader's Digest Road
Pleasantville, NY 10570-7000 USA

Copyright © 2010 by Amber Books, Ltd.
Produced by Amber Books Ltd., Bradley's Close
74–77 White Lion Street
London N1 9PF, U.K.

Amber Project Editor: James Bennett
Amber Designer: Joe Conneally

Gareth Stevens Executive Managing Editor: Lisa M. Herrington
Gareth Stevens Editor: Joann Jovinelly
Gareth Stevens Senior Designer: Keith Plechaty

Interior Images
All illustrations © Amber Books, Ltd., except:
Ancient Art & Architecture Collection: 19 (Prisma); Art Archive: 7 (Gianni Dagli Orti/National
Archaeological Museum, Athens); Bridgeman Art Library: 26t (Giraudon/Museo Archeologico
Nazionale, Naples), 26b (Alinari/Museo Archeologico Nazionale, Naples); Corbis: 3, 18
(Araldo de Luca), 21 (Herbert Spichtinger/Zefa); De Agostini Picture Library: 8 (A. Dagli Orti),
9 (G. Nimatallah), 13 (G. Dagli Orti), 20, 24 (G. Dagli Orti); Photos.com: 27; public domain: 4, 6

Cover Images
Front Cover: Left, bust of Leonidas (G. Dagli Orti/De Agostini Picture Library); top right, bronze
spearheads dating from the sixth century B.C. (G. Dagli Orti/De Agostini Picture Library); bottom
right, iron and gold breastplate (G. Dagli Orti/De Agostini Picture Library)
Back Cover: Center, parchment (James Steidl/Dreamstime); right, Greek hoplite (Amber Books)

Printed in the United States of America

1 2 3 4 5 6 7 8 9 13 12 11 10 09

Contents

CHAPTER 1

Fortress Cities

The ancient Greek **civilization** thrived 4,000 years ago. It included islands in the Aegean and Adriatic Seas. Greece's hot, dry climate and its harbors and mountains shaped its history. Only some areas in Greece had fertile land for growing crops.

Different cultures rose and fell in ancient Greece. Some of what we know about those cultures is based on facts. Other information is based on **legends**.

The ancient Greeks built **city-states**—strong, independent areas like small countries. They kept strong armies. They fought each other for the best land, but sometimes they worked together to fight a common enemy, such as the Persians.

Minoan Civilization

The earliest Greeks were Minoans, named after King Minos. The Minoans were sea traders. They lived on Crete, an island in the Aegean Sea, from about 3000 B.C. The Minoans produced grain and wine and traded with Egypt and Syria. They became rich and built palaces on Crete, some of which have been uncovered by

▼ **PALACE OF KNOSSOS**
The ruins of the palace of King Minos were discovered on the island of Crete in 1878. Some of the buildings have been rebuilt. They have also been painted in the colors that archaeologists think the Minoans used.

archaeologists. The Minoan civilization reached its peak around 2000 B.C., but then disappeared. Historians are not certain what happened. Some believe the Minoans may have disappeared due to a natural disaster.

The Greek **philosopher** Plato (429–347 B.C.) told a story about an island named Atlantis. He said that Atlantis disappeared in a single day. For years people thought Atlantis was a legend. Some historians believe the story of Atlantis is based on the disappearance of the Minoan civilization.

DID YOU KNOW?

Each city-state had its own laws. A man named Draco created most of the laws that governed the people of Athens. Draco's laws were so strict that today we say that a harsh rule is "draconian."

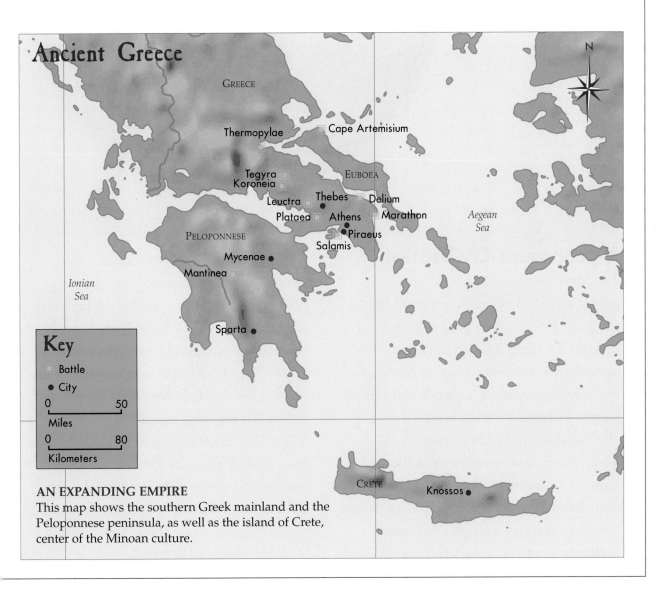

Ancient Greece

GREECE

Thermopylae · Cape Artemisium

Tegyra
Koroneia · EUBOEA

Leuctra · Thebes · Delium

Plataea · Athens · Marathon

PELOPONNESE · Piraeus

Salamis

Aegean Sea

Mycenae

Mantinea

Ionian Sea

Sparta

Key

▫ Battle
● City

0   50
Miles

0   80
Kilometers

CRETE · Knossos

AN EXPANDING EMPIRE
This map shows the southern Greek mainland and the Peloponnese peninsula, as well as the island of Crete, center of the Minoan culture.

This picture, painted on a drinking cup around 500 B.C., shows the Greek warrior Achilles (Ak-ILL-eze) bandaging the arm of his friend Patroclus (PAT-ro-kluss) during the Trojan War. Greek soldiers were inspired to be brave by images of the heroes of the Trojan War.

Mycenaean Civilization

The Mycenaean civilization came into power around 1500 B.C. They lived on the southern Peloponnese peninsula, part of mainland Greece. The Mycenaeans were named after Mycenae. Like the Minoans, they were sea traders. Legends claim that King Agamemnon ruled Mycenae.

Outsiders invaded Mycenae, so Mycenaeans built walls around the city, making it a **fortress**. They defended the city with **Bronze Age** weapons. Archaeologists have found those weapons and other **artifacts** at ancient Greek burial sites.

We know about the Mycenaeans from Homer, an ancient Greek poet. Homer's poems are likely based on battles between the Mycenaeans and the Trojans, another warrior culture, during the Trojan War (1194–1184 B.C.). Homer wrote **epics**, or long poems. The *Iliad* tells how King Agamemnon led the Mycenaeans against Troy in the Trojan War. The *Odyssey* recounts a decade-long journey taken by Odysseus on his return home from Troy. The Mycenaean civilization ended around 1100 B.C., bringing ancient Greece into a **Dark Age**, a period of disorganized fighting and decline.

City-States

The Dorians were a warrior civilization from northern Greece. Dorian invaders attacked the Mycenaeans, ending their power. At that time, various tribes formed scattered settlements. Over time, some settlements became city-states with military fortresses. City-states fought one another for territory and food. Some protected each other from invaders. Dorians, who stayed behind after the fall of Mycenae, governed several city-states, including Sparta.

The Spartans

The Dorians founded Sparta around 1100 B.C. They defeated the Messenians, a local farming tribe. After the defeat, the Spartans enslaved the Messenians and called them **helots**. The Spartans forced the helots to farm the land for them, but they feared the helots would revolt. To keep the helots enslaved, the Spartans raised their male children as soldiers to form a strong army.

All Spartan boys were trained to fight from age seven, when they were taken from their parents. They moved into dormitories

This Mycenaean dagger, or short sword, has a gold handle. Later Greeks told stories about the wealth of their Mycenaean ancestors.

The blade of this dagger is iron. Iron was easier to get than the copper and tin needed for bronze, but it was harder to shape.

◄ TROJAN TREASURE
People thought the stories of the Trojan War were just legends. A man named Heinrich Schliemann (SHLEE-mahn) believed Homer's tales were true. In the nineteenth century he went to Greece and Turkey and dug in places Homer mentioned in the *Iliad*. He may have found the ruins of Troy. He found treasures and weapons such as this **dagger**.

with older Spartan warriors. Spartan boys were trained to endure pain. They slept on reed mats, which they made themselves. The Spartans lived and ate together. Their food and clothing was plain. All of their energy was focused on fighting.

The Athenians

Athens was founded around the time of the Mycenaeans. It remained unconquered by the Dorians when they invaded Greece. Athens was located about 150 miles (241 kilometers) northeast of Sparta. Athens and Sparta became powerful. Those city-states were sometimes at war.

▼ **A BRONZE HELMET**
The Greeks made their armor and weapons out of bronze. That metal is a mixture of copper and tin. Bronze was easier to make than iron or steel, but it was not as strong.

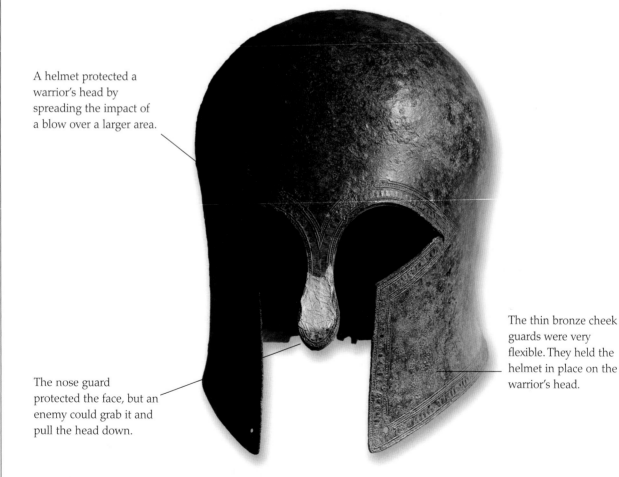

A helmet protected a warrior's head by spreading the impact of a blow over a larger area.

The thin bronze cheek guards were very flexible. They held the helmet in place on the warrior's head.

The nose guard protected the face, but an enemy could grab it and pull the head down.

Athens was the center of ancient Greek learning. It was also the birthplace of **democracy**. Although Athens was miles from the coast, its citizens expanded its territory to include a natural harbor at Piraeus, on the Aegean Sea. To protect that harbor, the Athenians built high walls that led from Athens to Piraeus.

Athens had many natural resources, including a silver mine. Its leaders made the silver into **currency**. The Athenians used that money to build warships. Athens' naval power would become its greatest strength.

The First Persian War

In 500 B.C., the Persians had a powerful **empire** in what is now Iraq and Iran. They fought the Greeks for years and tried to gain their territory. In 540 B.C., the Persians conquered several Greek city-states.

Beginning in 499 B.C., the Greeks revolted. The Athenians sent their army to help fight the Persians at sea, but were defeated. The victorious Persian King Darius decided to seek revenge against the Athenians. In 490 B.C., he landed his huge army at Marathon, near Athens.

▶ RUNNING INTO BATTLE
The Greeks believed in physical fitness. This was useful in war as well as in peace. At the battle of Marathon, the Athenian army ran the last mile to get close before the Persian archers could shoot. This wall painting from about 500 B.C. shows a Greek soldier running toward an enemy.

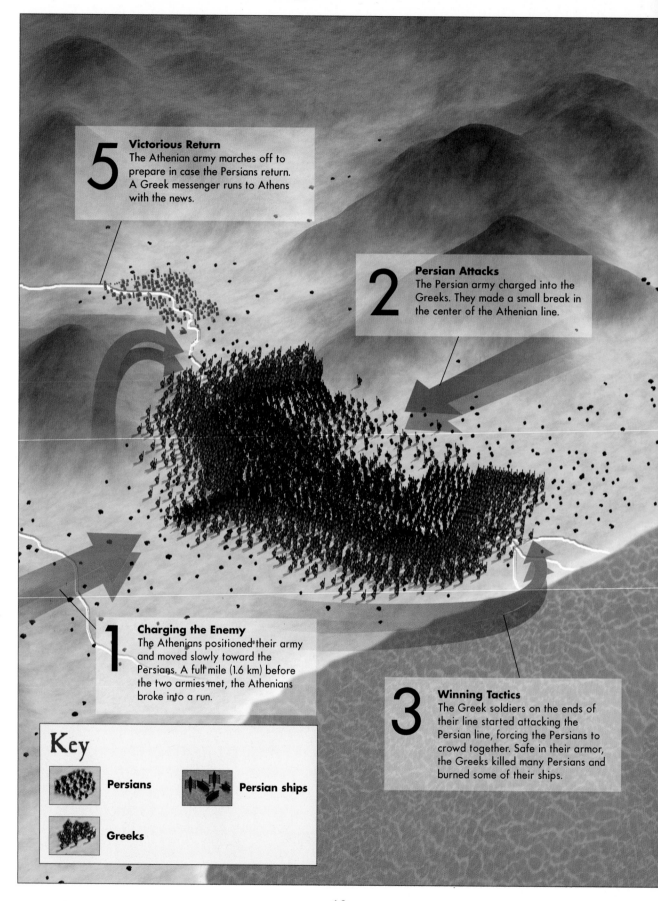

5 **Victorious Return**
The Athenian army marches off to prepare in case the Persians return. A Greek messenger runs to Athens with the news.

2 **Persian Attacks**
The Persian army charged into the Greeks. They made a small break in the center of the Athenian line.

1 **Charging the Enemy**
The Athenians positioned their army and moved slowly toward the Persians. A full mile (1.6 km) before the two armies met, the Athenians broke into a run.

3 **Winning Tactics**
The Greek soldiers on the ends of their line started attacking the Persian line, forcing the Persians to crowd together. Safe in their armor, the Greeks killed many Persians and burned some of their ships.

Key

Persians

Persian ships

Greeks

The Battle of Marathon

490 B.C.

The Persian army landed on the beaches of Marathon in September of 490 B.C., with a plan to capture Athens. The Athenians asked the Spartans for help, but they refused. The Athenian army fought the Persians alone.

The Persians had spearmen and archers at Marathon, which was 25 miles (40 km) from Athens. About 10,000 Greek foot soldiers faced a Persian force at least twice as large.

The Athenian general, Miltiades, ordered his soldiers to run the last mile toward the Persian ships. This would have been tough in armor that weighed about 70 pounds (32 kilograms).

The Athenians were spared death by their speed and armor, and they drove away the Persian fleet. A Greek legend says that a runner raced back to Athens with news of the victory, but then collapsed and died. That legend is the origin of the modern marathon race.

Persian Camp

4 Persians Flee to Sea
The remaining Persians headed to their ships and escaped out to sea. One-third of their army had been killed.

CHAPTER 2

War on Land

Ancient Greek foot soldiers were called **hoplites**. That name came from their **hoplons**, or shields. Hoplons were round wooden shields with painted images or letters that identified a soldier's city-state. Other Greek weapons and equipment were made from bronze. Protective armor had to be made thick, so it was heavy. Hoplites who could afford armor fought in the front line. That was

the deadliest position. For protection, they wore breastplates, **greaves** (leg guards), and helmets. Unarmored soldiers filled in the back. Hoplites also used slings, bows, and double-ended spears.

The Phalanx

Hoplite foot soldiers fought in a **phalanx**. That was a formation made up of many rows of men packed tightly, with their

Greek hoplites carried spears and swords for stabbing at close range.

The crests on the helmets were made of horsehair.

The Greek letter Λ on their shields is the equivalent of "L." It stands for Lacedemon (La-see-day-MON), the ancient name for Sparta.

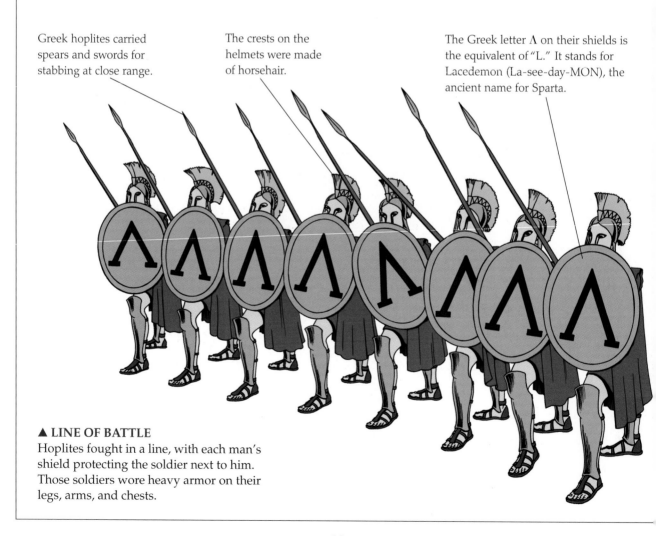

▲ LINE OF BATTLE
Hoplites fought in a line, with each man's shield protecting the soldier next to him. Those soldiers wore heavy armor on their legs, arms, and chests.

The soldier who owned this shield drew pictures of animals on the back. They may have been to remind him of his farm at home while he was away fighting.

This is the back of an early Greek shield. The soldier would have held the handle in the middle. If a Greek warrior was killed, he was traditionally carried home on his own shield.

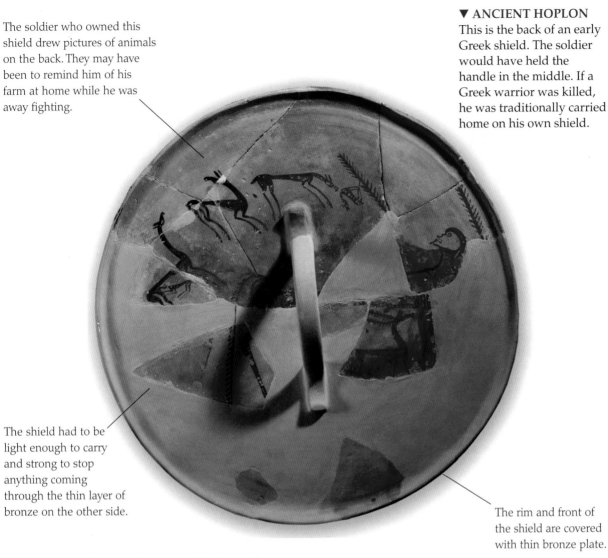

The shield had to be light enough to carry and strong to stop anything coming through the thin layer of bronze on the other side.

The rim and front of the shield are covered with thin bronze plate.

spear points facing forward. Each soldier protected the man to the right of him with his shield. The men in the back rows of the phalanx could not reach the enemy, so they fought by pushing the others forward.

The hoplites charged the enemy with great force. They tried to kill as many men as they could in the first clash. Then they pushed the enemy back. Anyone who fell could be trampled to death. If the phalanx was pushed hard enough, it broke apart. Soldiers in a broken phalanx had to run away quickly or risk being killed.

In Their Own Words

"It is a fine thing for a brave man to die when he has fallen among the front ranks while fighting for his homeland…. Make the spirit in your heart strong [but] do not be in love with life when you are a fighting man."

—Tyrtaeus, an ancient Greek poet, 700 B.C.

13

▲ **THROW AND RUN**
A peltast could run in and out of battle faster than a hoplite. Peltasts threw their javelins on the run to make them fly farther. They did not have the heavy armor of the hoplites, so they were able to run faster.

Early battles were short. Few people died, though those who did were often skilled soldiers. Sometimes, instead of fighting directly, hoplites marched through enemy territory destroying crops.

Peltasts

The phalanx worked well only against enemies in front of it. Once an enemy surrounded the phalanx, the hoplites usually lost the battle. To prevent themselves from being surrounded, lightly armed soldiers called **peltasts** guarded the sides of the phalanx.

Helmets and shields also provided protection for peltasts. They defended themselves by throwing javelins. They ran faster than hoplites because their equipment was lighter, so they had a better chance to escape.

Other Troops

Some hoplites and peltasts also carried short daggers. Foot soldiers from Crete were famous archers, while those from Rhodes were known for their ability to use the sling. Poor, unarmored foot soldiers or slaves were called **psiloi**. They fought only by throwing stones.

A few soldiers fought on horseback, but they were rare. Although Greek legends mention chariots, few were used in ancient Greece because the ground was too uneven.

14

Catapults

The ancient Greeks designed clever weapons. One shot arrows with such force that they could go through a shield. The Greek words for this weapon were *kata peltehs*, which give us our word **catapult**. It was invented around 400 B.C. Later catapults were mounted on ships.

The Greek mathematician and inventor Archimedes (287–212 B.C.) designed a very large catapult. It fired a 172-pound (78-kg) rock at the walls of enemy cities. Archimedes also designed other weapons, including a steam-powered cannon. When laying siege to a city, the Greeks used flamethrowers and **battering rams**.

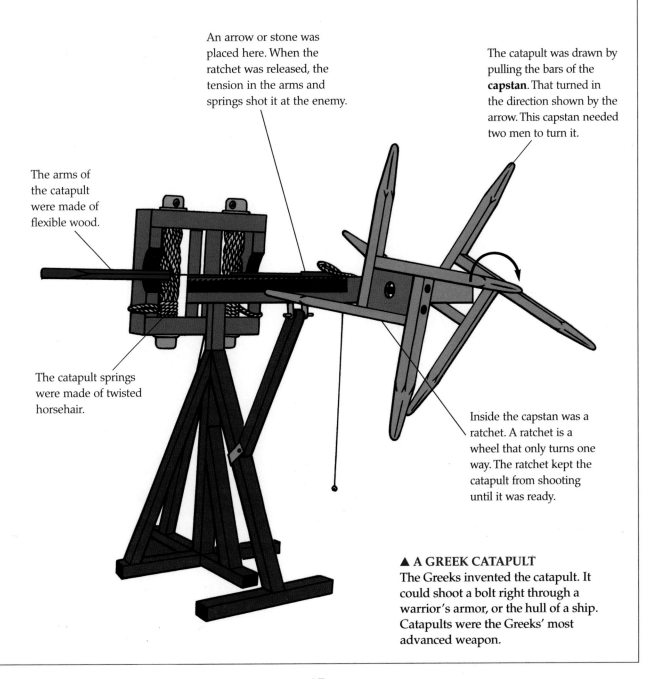

An arrow or stone was placed here. When the ratchet was released, the tension in the arms and springs shot it at the enemy.

The catapult was drawn by pulling the bars of the **capstan**. That turned in the direction shown by the arrow. This capstan needed two men to turn it.

The arms of the catapult were made of flexible wood.

The catapult springs were made of twisted horsehair.

Inside the capstan was a ratchet. A ratchet is a wheel that only turns one way. The ratchet kept the catapult from shooting until it was ready.

▲ A GREEK CATAPULT
The Greeks invented the catapult. It could shoot a bolt right through a warrior's armor, or the hull of a ship. Catapults were the Greeks' most advanced weapon.

War at Sea

Sailing was the easiest method of traveling in ancient Greece. The Greeks were talented ship builders, but they did not like to navigate in open seas. They sailed only along the coast or near the Greek islands.

The ancient Greeks feared pirates, since the thieves attacked and robbed coastal cities and merchant ships. Pirates stole valuables. They also kidnapped people and sold them as slaves. The Athenian navy became skilled at fighting pirates because they wanted to safeguard the sea trade that made Athens rich.

DID YOU KNOW?

Athens was built on a hill away from the coast to help protect it from pirates. High walls that created a waterway passage connected Athens to the coast, ending at the port of Piraeus. Enemies couldn't capture Athens or put the city under siege because food was imported by ship through the passage.

▼ A BRONZE RAM

This is an illustration of a bronze ram. It is similar to one found off the coast of Israel. It probably fell off a Greek ship during a voyage. This ram weighed half a ton. Rams such as this were very expensive and hard to make.

Rams were made of bronze because it does not rust in salt water. Today's ship propellers are often made of bronze.

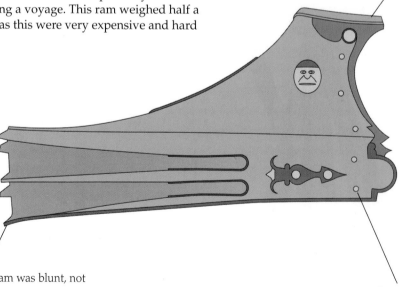

The front of the ram was blunt, not sharp. The Greeks did not want the ram to get stuck in the hull of the ship it had hit. That might sink their own ship.

Bolts ran through the ram and through the ship to hold the ram in place.

The stern ornament sheltered the helmsman and looked like a dolphin's tail.

A trireme had three rows of oarsmen. The oarsmen in the top row had longer oars than those at the bottom, so they could reach the water.

▲ **FAST AND DEADLY**
A Greek trireme using both oars and sails was the fastest ship in the ancient world. The Athenians kept two of their fastest triremes for sending emergency messages across the Aegean Sea.

Warships

The ancient Greeks sailed in long black ships with oars called **penteconters**. Later warships were **biremes**. Those were shorter and held two levels of rowers, with half of the men on higher benches.

The Greeks built bronze-plated battering rams on the ends of their ships. Those weapons knocked apart the planks of an enemy's hull so it took in water and risked sinking. Warships carried soldiers called **marines**. The marines and archers fought with the enemy's marines, often jumping aboard enemy ships to capture them.

Around 605 B.C., the Greeks built a faster warship, called the **trireme**, because it held three levels of rowers. With more manpower, triremes moved swiftly and were easier to control. A fast moving trireme was very difficult to ram.

Rowing the triremes was hard work. It was a skilled job that required strength and energy. The ships were crowded. Many rowers were hurt or drowned if another ship slammed against them.

Athenian Navy

Frequent sea trade helped Athens become a major economic power. Merchant ships needed protection from pirates. The Athenians were also concerned that the Persians would seek revenge on Athens.

"Athenians and the resident foreigners of military age should board the 200 triremes which have been made ready and resist the [Persians] in defense of their own freedom and that of the other Greeks…."

—Themistocles, leader of Athens, 480 B.C.

In 483 B.C., an Athenian leader named Themistocles convinced the Athenians to build a fleet of 200 triremes. His goal was to defend Athens from the Persians who he feared would return. The Athenians made their richest citizens pay for each trireme and its expenses. Poor Athenian citizens became crewmembers. Soon Athens had a large and powerful navy.

The Second Persian War

Themistocles was correct. In 480 B.C., the Persian leader, King Xerxes, ordered his army to invade Greece. The Persians so outnumbered the Greeks that many surrendered quickly, including the Macedonians from the north. Despite their surrender, the Macedonians continued to help those Greeks who wanted to fight.

Greek warships were long, low, and fast. They could catch and destroy the pirates' captured merchant ships, which were mostly powered by sails.

Pirates captured merchant ships and used them to carry off their **plunder**. In this painting, the pirates are getting ready to fight as the warship draws near.

▶ **ROBBERS ON THE SEA**
The painting on this bowl shows marines in the Greek ship on the left ready to attack the pirate ship at right. The small ships of the pirates were no match for a strong navy like that of Athens.

The Athenians and Spartans chose to fight under Themistocles' leadership. The Greeks decided to try to stop the Persians before they could get into southern Greece.

Persians Destroy Athens

King Leonidas of Sparta and his men slowed the Persian army at the pass of Thermopylae. The Greeks fighting there were killed, but they had given other Greek soldiers more time to prepare. At the same time, about 270 Greek triremes fought the Persians off Cape Artemisium on the island of Euboea. The Persian fleet was much larger, however, and the Greek navy was lucky to escape.

The Persians then headed south toward Athens. They burned Athens to the ground, though most Athenians had escaped to the island of Salamis. The Greeks and Persians fought a second naval battle near Salamis. The Greek triremes tricked the Persian ships to sail into a narrow area of water near the island. That passage became so crowded that the ships' oars got in each other's way. The Greek ships suddenly charged the Persian ships. The Greeks crushed the oars of some Persian ships,

leaving them stranded, or sank them completely. Xerxes responded by taking most of his army back to Persia to prevent it from getting cut off by the Greek fleet.

The Athenian Empire

The Athenians and Persians continued fighting. Eventually, in 478 B.C., the Athenians formed a group of city-states. They called it the **Delian League**. Its goals were to protect Greeks from future invasions by Persia, to seek revenge against Persia, and to divide the spoils of war. The Delian League became an Athenian empire.

CHAPTER 4

The Greeks at War

The Athenian Delian League fought the Spartan **Peloponnesian League** (the Spartans and their allies from the Peloponnese) in the Peloponnesian War (431–404 B.C.).

Throughout the war, neither side had weapons that could easily capture walled cities. Instead, armies placed cities under siege, hoping to starve their citizens into surrender. Just such a siege happened northwest of Athens in 429 B.C. when the Spartans took Plataea. Another battle occurred at Delium in 424 B.C. In that contest, the Athenians won by using a flamethrower to set fire to the city. A truce was made between Athens and Sparta, but some of their allies kept fighting. Before long, the war started again without a clear victory.

Island Fortress

In 415 B.C., the Athenians decided to conquer Syracuse, a powerful city-state on the island of Sicily. They went there to defend their allies. The Athenians believed that if they won

◀ OFF TO WAR
Greek soldiers had to stay in step and close together as they marched toward the enemy. If there was a space in the line, the enemy soldiers could get behind the shields with their swords.

550 B.C.

500 B.C.

540–499 Persia invades Greek city-states in Asia. City-states revolt against Persian rule.

490 Battle of Marathon
480 Battles of Thermopylae, Cape Artemisium, and Salamis

PERSIAN WARS

► WEALTHY SYRACUSE
Tyrants like Dionysius of Syracuse took much of their cities' money. Dionysius used the cash to build huge open air theaters like this one. He also used the money to pay engineers and inventors to build new weapons.

Sicily they would be strong enough to defeat the Spartans once and for all.

The Athenians attacked Syracuse with 5,000 soldiers, and its people asked Sparta for help. The Spartans could spare few men or weapons. However, the Spartans were such skilled fighters that they disrupted the siege of Syracuse by attacking an Athenian fort. The Spartans also fought the Athenians at sea and took their fleet. Eventually, the Spartans stopped the siege. Syracuse was saved. Once the Athenian fleet was destroyed, Athens lost its strength. Sparta became the most powerful city-state.

Inventive Tyrant

At the time of the attack, Syracuse was ruled by Dionysius. He had seized power by force. He was known for being a cruel and ruthless tyrant. He wanted to capture the nearby city of Motya. Knowing how difficult it was to take a defended city, Dionysius hired wise men to help him. They made high towers on wheels to help

DID YOU KNOW?

When an army turned and ran, the victors set up a *trophy*, from the Greek word for *turn*. The trophy was a set of the losing side's armor on a tree trunk in the shape of a soldier. The trophy reminded both sides of who had won the battle.

400 B.C. **350** B.C. **300** B.C.

415 Siege of Syracuse   **394** Battle of Koroneia   **362** Battle of Mantinea   **336** Alexander rules Macedonia.
429 Siege of Plataea   **375** Battle of Tegyra   **331** Battle of Gaugamela
424 Battle of Delium   **371** Battle of Leuctra   **323** Death of Alexander

PELOPONNESIAN WAR   ALEXANDER THE GREAT

the Syracusans climbed Motya's walls and entered the city. The wise men also built catapults. With those weapons, Dionysius took Motya in 397 B.C. Soon all Greeks were using catapults and siege towers.

Sparta's Wars

Sparta ruled Greece for more than 30 years. They dealt harshly with Athenians and their allies. Those who did not hand over territory were attacked.

Some Greek city-states continued fighting Sparta. At the battle of Koroneia in 394 B.C., the phalanxes of Thebes and Sparta crashed into each other so hard that all the spears broke. Men on both sides fought with daggers. After ongoing fighting, the Spartans were driven out of several city-states. They responded by declaring a war with Thebes.

At the battle of Tegyra in 375 B.C., a small force of Thebans beat a larger Spartan army. The Thebans moved at an angle across the battlefield and defeated the Spartans by smashing through their line.

Light catapults called scorpions were used from the highest holes in the tower.

Iron plates protected the tower from enemy catapults and fire. There were water tanks inside to put out any fires.

Big catapults in the tower's base hurled stones that were large enough to damage the city's walls.

The siege tower was moved into place on strong wheels.

◄ A GIANT WAR MACHINE
This siege tower was used to attack the island city of Rhodes in 305–304 B.C. Soldiers inside the tower were protected as they approached the walls of the city. Great rams tried to knock down the walls. The Rhodians trapped the tower in a mud pit they made by opening their sewers next to the wall.

In 371 B.C., a Spartan army met a Theban force near Leuctra. Despite their earlier defeat, the Spartans thought they were untouchable. Again the Thebans formed a deep phalanx and smashed through Spartan troops.

Thebes Leads Greece

After that defeat, Thebes became the leading city-state of Greece. Although other city-states continued fighting, the Thebans weakened Sparta. Spartan control over Greece ended.

As the Thebans gained power, they formed partnerships. Other city-states, such as Athens, joined Sparta to resist Thebes. At the battle of Mantinea in 362 B.C., Thebes' best general was killed. Even so, Sparta's forces were defeated. By then, however, both sides were weakened. With many of its leaders dead, southern Greece became vulnerable to attack. The powerful Macedonians to the north invaded Greece in 338 B.C. and easily absorbed southern Greece into the Macedonian empire.

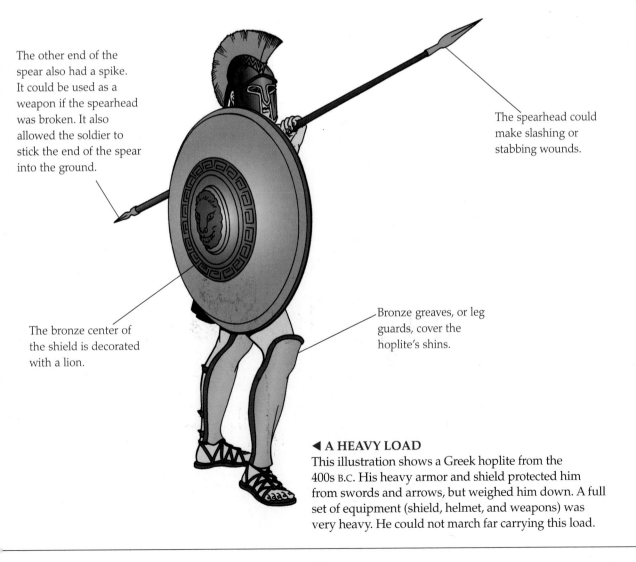

The other end of the spear also had a spike. It could be used as a weapon if the spearhead was broken. It also allowed the soldier to stick the end of the spear into the ground.

The spearhead could make slashing or stabbing wounds.

The bronze center of the shield is decorated with a lion.

Bronze greaves, or leg guards, cover the hoplite's shins.

◀ **A HEAVY LOAD**
This illustration shows a Greek hoplite from the 400s B.C. His heavy armor and shield protected him from swords and arrows, but weighed him down. A full set of equipment (shield, helmet, and weapons) was very heavy. He could not march far carrying this load.

CHAPTER 5

Alexander the Great

King Philip II of Macedon (382–336 B.C.) wanted to become a great ruler. He knew that southern Greece had been weakened by years of fighting. Using money from mines near his kingdom, King Philip outfitted his army with catapults and extra long spears called **sarissas**. His was the most well equipped army in the world.

Philip and his army moved down into Greece itself, overtaking city-states as they went. An assassin killed Philip, and his son Alexander became the king of Macedonia.

▼ AN IRON VEST

This is a **cuirass** (KWEE-rahs), which was worn to protect the chest. Regular soldiers in Alexander's time wore cuirasses made from layers of linen cloth glued together. Iron gave more protection than linen, but was much heavier and more expensive. Alexander himself wore a cuirass like this one, which came from the tomb of a Macedonian king.

This plate protected the soldier's neck.

The iron plates were decorated with gold. The gold has not rusted like the iron. It looks exactly as it did when it was new.

The cuirass was pulled on over the soldier's head. A linen cuirass also fastened around the waist.

Because it was hard to get close to them, the men in the phalanx wore less armor. This meant that they could march faster.

A man positioned in the rear kept his sarissa raised high to protect against stones and arrows thrown by enemy soldiers.

The shield the Macedonians used was smaller and lighter than the big one the Greeks had.

▲ **MILITARY FORCE**
The Macedonian phalanx helped Alexander win all his battles. With their long sarissas, his soldiers were almost unbeatable if they stayed in formation.

Alexander was possibly the greatest military leader the world has ever known. He not only led the Greeks, but he admired and adopted the Greek language and lifestyle. Alexander spread Greek culture throughout his growing empire.

Alexander Takes Over

Alexander put his infantry into a huge phalanx larger than the Greeks had ever used. He also armed his cavalry with lances like the infantry's long sarissas. In 336 B.C., Alexander led his army toward Persia.

DID YOU KNOW?

Alexander had a group of friends who were his bodyguards. Alexander ate, drank, and fought beside them. One friend, Cleitus, saved Alexander's life at the battle of Granicus. A few years later, however, Alexander killed Cleitus with a spear during an argument.

While Alexander had his sights set on Persia, Thebes revolted. Alexander quickly marched back and destroyed the city.

The Persian king, Darius III, was a good leader, but a poor general. In 334 B.C., Alexander defeated the Persian army at the Granicus River. Both armies clashed again in a narrow canyon near Issus, but the Persians were again defeated.

▼ ▶ A FEARLESS CHALLENGER

This mosaic was created around 130 years after the death of Alexander, and gives a dramatic picture of a battle between the Greeks and the Persians. It was discovered in the ruins of Pompeii, the Roman town buried by volcanic ash in A.D. 79. Alexander (right and below left) charges straight at the Persian King Darius III (below right).

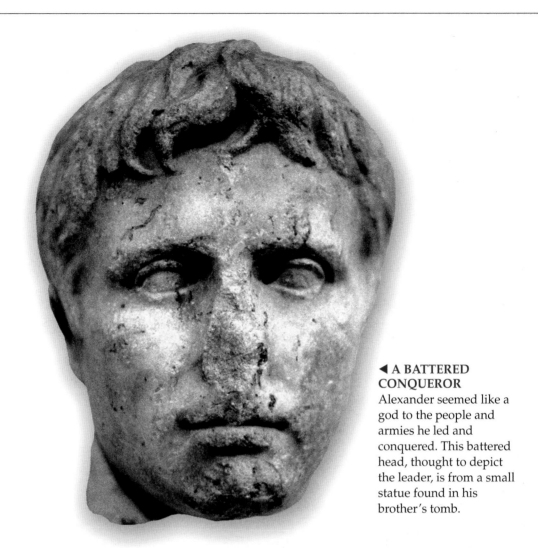

◀ **A BATTERED CONQUEROR**
Alexander seemed like a god to the people and armies he led and conquered. This battered head, thought to depict the leader, is from a small statue found in his brother's tomb.

Alexander Conquers the World

Alexander turned his attention from Persia and traveled to North Africa, where he conquered Phoenicia and Egypt. He founded a city in Egypt, which he named Alexandria, and turned it into a center of Greek culture. In the meantime, Darius was preparing to fight Alexander's army again.

Darius collected a huge army of soldiers, elephants, and cavalry. He built chariots with sharp blades on them and waited for Alexander to return from Egypt. But the Persians were no match for Alexander's

DID YOU KNOW?

When he died, Alexander the Great was only 32 years old. He had conquered most of the world as it was known to the ancient Greeks. His military successes have inspired many leaders throughout history, including Napoleon Bonaparte and Adolf Hitler.

In Their Own Words

"Now, a tomb is enough for someone who thought the whole world was not enough."

—Thought to have been the inscription on Alexander the Great's tomb

army. In 331 B.C., Alexander defeated Darius again at Gaugamela.

Alexander proclaimed himself the new king of Persia. He led his army through Afghanistan and into India, but his men grew tired. After a short campaign in South Asia, Alexander's army wanted only to return to Greece.

By 323 B.C., Alexander and his army returned to Babylon. He had been wounded many times over the years, and now he was sick. A short time later, Alexander died.

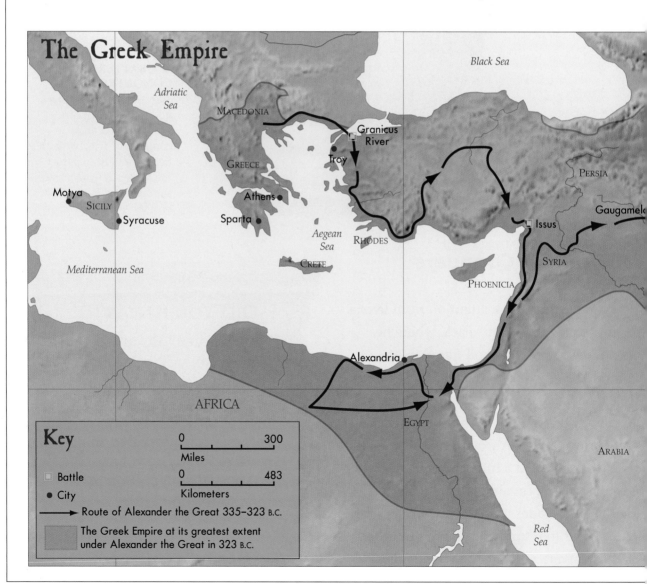

The Greek Empire

Adriatic Sea
Black Sea
MACEDONIA
Granicus River
GREECE
Troy
PERSIA
Motya
SICILY
Athens
Gaugamela
Syracuse
Sparta
Issus
Aegean Sea
RHODES
SYRIA
CRETE
PHOENICIA
Mediterranean Sea
Alexandria
AFRICA
EGYPT
ARABIA

Key

0 — 300
Miles
0 — 483
Kilometers

▫ Battle
● City
→ Route of Alexander the Great 335–323 B.C.

The Greek Empire at its greatest extent under Alexander the Great in 323 B.C.

Red Sea

After Alexander

After Alexander's death, his empire was divided among his three generals. Around 200 B.C., the Romans began fighting the Greeks. By 31 B.C., all Greek city-states were under Roman leadership.

We remember the Greeks for their art, literature, and ideas. The Spartans in particular are remembered for their bravery in battle. Alexander the Great was among history's greatest leaders who spread Greek culture throughout the world.

▼ **ROUTE OF ALEXANDER THE GREAT**
The ancient Greek civilization began around the southern mainland of Greece and the Peloponnese peninsula. Later, Greek city-states were founded on the coast of what is now Turkey. In the 330s B.C., the Macedonian king Alexander the Great expanded the Greek Empire. He led his armies deep into the Middle East and as far as India, spreading Greek culture and ideas.

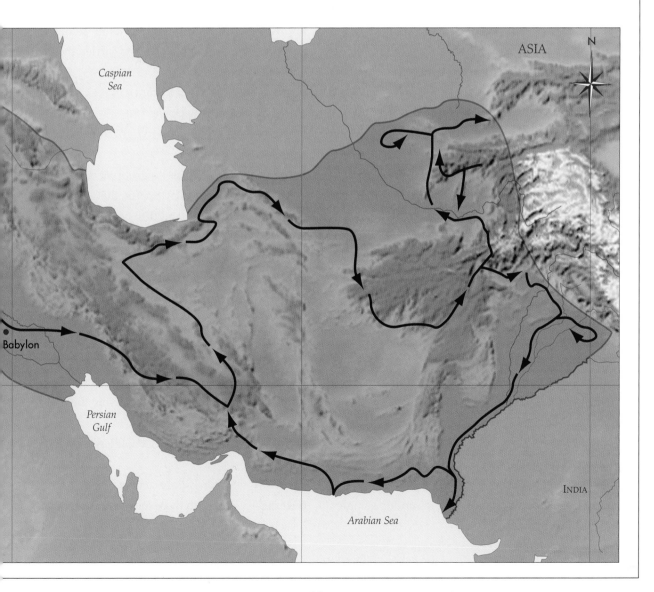

Glossary

archaeologists—people who study human history by digging up and studying the remains of earlier civilizations

artifacts—objects made by humans

battering rams—large wooden or metal poles used for smashing walls, doors, and the hulls of ships

biremes—ships with two levels of rowers on each side

Bronze Age—the period in history between the Stone Age and the Iron Age, when weapons and tools began to be made from bronze. In Europe this was between 2300 and 600 B.C.

capstan—a wheel used for winding a rope or cable

catapult—a machine powered by tension, used for throwing objects

city-states—independent regions with their own governments and armies, centered around a single city such as Athens

civilization—the people of a particular area and their society, way of life, and culture

cuirass—a piece of armor protecting the chest and back

currency—the money used in a region or state

dagger—a short sword used for stabbing

Dark Age—a period in which a civilization develops slowly or declines, and about which little information is known

Delian League—a group of ancient Greek city-states, led by Athens, against the Persians between 478 and 404 B.C., and against the Spartans between 377 and 338 B.C.

democracy—a system of government in which people vote in elections for representatives who govern on their behalf

empire—a region or group of states under a single supreme authority or ruler

epics—long poems, normally passed down through history by word of mouth, that tell the stories of legendary heroes or the ancient history of a people or civilization

fortress—a well-defended military camp or fortified town occupied by soldiers

greaves—leather, wooden, or metal guards that protect a soldier's lower legs

helots—the name the Spartans gave to the Messenians after they had defeated them and made them slaves

hoplites—heavily armored Greek foot soldiers

hoplons—round wooden shields carried by Greek foot soldiers

legends—stories about the ancient past that may not have actually happened

marines—soldiers trained to fight from and on board ships

Peloponnesian League—a group of city-states in the Peloponnese, led by Sparta, that worked together in the sixth and fifth centuries B.C.

peltasts—lightly armored foot soldiers who carried javelins

penteconters—ancient Greek warships with 50 oars

phalanx—a group of foot soldiers in formation, with shields overlapping and long spears held upright

philosopher—a person who studies the underlying truths of knowledge, reality, and existence

plunder—property gained illegally by theft or violence

psiloi—poor, unarmored foot soldiers who fought only with stones

sarissas—very long spears carried by foot soldiers

trireme—a ship with three levels of rowers on each side

For More Information

Books

Ancient Greece. Life Long Ago (series). Tea Benduhn (Weekly Reader, 2007)

Ancient Greece. Passport to the Past (series). Richard Tames (Rosen Publishing, 2009)

The Conquests of Alexander the Great. Pivotal Moments in History (series). Alison Behnke (Twenty-First Century Books, 2007)

I Wonder Why Greeks Built Temples and Other Questions about Ancient Greece. I Wonder Why (series). Fiona MacDonald (Kingfisher, 2006)

Life In Ancient Athens. Picture the Past (series). Jane Shuter (Heinemann, 2005)

Thucydides. Biography from Ancient Civilizations (series). Jim Whiting (Mitchell Lane Publishers, 2008)

You Wouldn't Want To Be In Alexander the Great's Army!: Miles You'd Rather Not March. You Wouldn't Want to… (series). Jacqueline Morley (Children's Press, 2005)

Ancient Greece

http://greece.mrdonn.org
Learn more about ancient Greece, the daily lifestyles of its people, the different Greek city-states, and the legend of the Trojan Horse.

Ancient-Greece.org

http://www.ancient-greece.org
Discover ancient Greece through its archaeology, architecture, and art on this web site that includes maps of the ancient world, photos of artifacts, and a time line.

The Ancient City of Athens

http://www.stoa.org/athens
Take a tour of ancient Athens on this web site that includes diagrams of the city-state, including the Acropolis.

Ancient Greek Civilizations

http://www.mnsu.edu/emuseum/prehistory/aegean
Read more about ancient Greece on this web site that includes a detailed history of the civilization as well as photos of ancient artifacts.

The Ancient Greeks

http://www.kidspast.com/world-history/0058-ancient-greeks.php
Explore ancient Greece while learning fun facts on this web site that also features craft projects and online activities.

Web Sites

Publisher's note to educators and parents: Our editors have carefully reviewed these web sites to ensure that they are suitable for children. Many web sites change frequently, however, and we cannot guarantee that a site's future contents will continue to meet our high standards of quality and educational value. Be advised that children should be closely supervised whenever they access the Internet.

Index

About the Author

Dr. Rob S. Rice is a Professor in the Department of Naval History at the American Military University. He has a Ph.D in Ancient History from the University of Pennsylvania. He is the author of sections of several other books including the *Oxford Companion to American Military History*, *Battles of the Ancient World*, and *Battles of the Bible*.